Between the Motion and the Act

ISBN 978-0-6151-3896-1

Cover design by Melanie E. Williams

I dedicate this book to my mother, Aline; the one who wore the *Grape Cape*. To my son, Dorian who makes my heart dance with uncut joy. Keep your soul beautiful. And to my father, Richard...you are now the angel who watches over me.

To my *Angel Friend*, this one's for you too.

Table of Contents

Acknowledgements – 5

Struggles – 6

Lessons Learned – 22

Gratitude and Victory – 38

People You Know – 57

Something to Relate To – 71

It's Just a Fantasy – 92

Index – 107

Acknowledgements

To God who bestowed upon me the gift of arranging words to evoke emotion. I thank you for allowing it to speak for me.

To my family and friends that believed I could go one mile more, I thank you and I love you.

To all people, from every land, all walks of life, and every period of time past, present, and future...

Melanie E. Williams

Struggles

Bagged Dreams
Beatings behind My Fence
Cocooned
Dehumanized
Faded Expression
Falling With Frailty
Krazed
Loveless Vertigo
Not With My Tears
Ode to a Lonely Soul
Peer
Sailing upon a Lover's Titanic
Subjugation
What He Gets At Night
Woman's Sorrow Part One

"It is never too late to be what you might have been."

-George Eliot

Bagged Dreams

She packed up her dreams and threw them into a plastic
bag...every last wish she ever had.

Slung them into a can like yesterday's news...
Hand slapping hand. She was through.

One look back, two, and then three
A moment of hesitation and then she walked away from
destiny.

Melanie E. Williams

A person's worth in this world is estimated
according to the value they put on themselves."

-Jean De La Bruyere

Beatings behind My Fence

The beatings behind my fence can never be ignored
The life behind that fence will take time to be restored

I wonder if she knows I hear her cries late at night?
How visions play in my mind as he pounds her in mere sight?

Voices break as his fist is drawing near
I wonder if she knows I feel
the fear that she hates to fear?

Imagine her children watching with wild, frightened eyes
As the beast consumes their mother, it devours
their shattered lives

I pray comfort will soon cross the path of she
Guide her to a reawakening so she can live freely

To know that genuine love requires
no bruises, blood, or stains
The ultimate love brings peace
that forever remains unchanged
So, allow the beatings to continue no more
No timid children, no screaming woman
crouched down on the floor
No cries of fear, no voices in pain
No blows to land, no control to gain

No brutal lies, no beatings in the light
No silent onlookers in the darkness of night
No blood to be shed, no clothes colored red
No babies screaming instead of resting in bed

No more beatings behind my fence!

"I only ask to be free.
The butterflies are free."

-Charles Dickens

Cocooned

A small beautiful girl; barely age eleven
cast her eyes to the sky because somewhere up in heaven...
Roamed a pair of powerful eyes
with a scope far and wide
That sees the torment she suffers each day;
from the might of the hand that brought her this way.

"I wonder if God forgot I was here?"
She whispers to herself through a thunderstorm of tears.
But for her, the blue skies have now clouded to gray;
another day in dark silence, God has passed her way.
"But where was His loving, saving power?"
The little girl moaned to herself hour after hour?

As the time ticked her body soon fell weak
"It's been days now God, since I've had some sleep."
She uttered in silence in fear of the one
that battered and bruised 'till all was said and done.
And then without notice, an angel appeared
"It's ok. Listen to me. There's nothing to fear.

With the passage of each year, God has heard your
prayers, felt your sorrow, felt your pain.
So by the might of HIS HAND, your life you'll regain."
That little girl, now a woman, fell down to her knees
and HE lifted her up with great care and ease.
With her chin in HIS hand, HE held her head high
"The torture is now over. You may live. Dry your eyes."

Melanie E. Williams

"Whilst shame kept its watch, virtue is not wholly extinguished in the heart."

-Edmund Burke

Dehumanized

You make my head hang low every time you are near
Instill within my spirit a fear I loathe to fear

Rob me of my dignity in the presence of your friends
Never cared about the bleeding of my heart deep within

You make my head hang low when you joke at my expense
This disregard for my humanity is deeply intense

"However long the night, the dawn will break."

-African Proverb

Faded Expression

Have you seen my smile?
I lost it along life's way
Somewhere amidst my experiences
my smile has faded away

Disappeared without a trace
a sweet expression cannot be found
Living is oh so sullen
without a gentle smile around

Maybe it was stolen
from underneath my nose
and placed in a world
were smiles no one can know

Could it be that I've allowed it
to be taken by someone I loved?
I'm in search of an expression
I was once proud of

Have you seen my smile?
The one that belongs to me
I need to find some tranquility
so that my spirit can be free

Melanie E. Williams

"There are two kinds of weakness; that which
breaks and that which bends."

-James Russell Lowell

Falling With Frailty

I remembered as if it were yesterday
The night he returned and my decision swayed

Truthfully, I longed to resist his plea
But my heart softened when he
whispered, "Baby, what about you and me?"

"I can't do this again
And besides, you came with her."
"Her? It's for you that I care."

As he worked to subdue me with sweet memories we created
"To be or not to be?" was the question I debated

Subsequently, I became weak and fell under his touch
In the depths of my soul, I wanted him as much

"Love blinds all men alike, both the reasonable
and the foolish."

-Menander of Athens

Krazed

Have you ever loved someone that made you feel...krazed?
Who affixed such an emotion upon you like a glaze?

Distorted your reality... and left you in a haze?
See, only intense lovers understand this kind of kraze

Ok, allow me to explain.... in a few words paraphrased
To be caught in this amour, keeps you to-tal-ly amazed

Your mind is aflutter and your heart... is ablaze
Except... this kind of kraze turns its lover into prey

You'll find yourself thinking of him night and day
Heavily upon your mind this sordid love will weigh

Although it's a dark love-- to you its light rays
What a very, very sad situation
to be a victim of love's kraze

Because unknowingly it beguiles
and your love it will slay

Melanie E. Williams

"No excellent soul is exempt from a mixture of madness."

-Aristotle

Loveless Vertigo

Crazy to think this was true romance
When the very one I adored was a fallen man

How could I not understand that he loved me not?
Oh, now I remember...it was because the sex was so hot!

Did you know I couldn't see the forest
because I saw no trees?
Yeah, I was confused to think this was forever
when it was only temporary

I found myself at the feet of a man already down
Gentle with his touch, yes
but inside no love was around

Sad to see just how crazy I loved him so,
But overjoyed I'm no longer caught
in his loveless vertigo

"There is sacredness in tears. They are not the mark
of weakness, but of power... They are the messengers
of overwhelming grief, of deep contrition,
and of unspeakable love."

-Washington Irving

Not with My Tears

Not...with my tears have you ever cried
Under the misty warmth of clouded skies

In a lonely bed without someone to hold
With each passing year as I grow old

As I wrestle with a screaming silence inside my head
Dowwwn flows the sorrow that I dread

Not! With my tears have you quivered in pain
As I ached to see you once again

Addicted to a love that cannot grow
So my eyes become filled with tears that slooowly flow

Not with my tears...does your spirit feel weak
Reminiscing about a love made in July's heat

Longing to taste... the sweetness... in your lips
Desiring to feel the passion in your grip

If only with your eyes and your heart could you cry
To understand what I feel so deep inside

...but not with my tears

Melanie E. Williams

"She dwelt among the untrodden ways beside the
springs of dove. A maid whom there were none
to praise and very few to love."

-William Wordsworth

Ode to a Lonely Soul

Ode to a lonely soul that silently weeps away
No one questions her emotions; a rescue delayed

Mute is her language because there are no ears
Hazed is her expression because there's no more tears

Blindness provides no vision; the eyes cannot see
An insane force of gloom; her warm familiarity

A touch cold
Memories faded
Mind sold
Reality jaded

Answers are out of reach because she's far away
For her there is no tomorrow; it's just another day

"The eye is the mirror of the soul."

-Proverb

Peer

Look into my eyes
I want to peek into your soul
Define what you are saying
because your truth remains untold

Let me see your eyes and
remember the beauty they possess
To never forget silent messages
they say with tenderness

If you let me see your eyes
I can understand your pain
Now look into my windows, my love
Can't you see we are the same?

Please, let me peer into your soul
because you're so beautiful to me
Are you so afraid to look and let
your spirit be set free?

Melanie E. Williams

"The human heart is like a ship on a stormy sea driven
about by winds blowing from all four corners of heaven."

-Martin Luther

Sailing upon a Lover's Titanic

Somehow you knew that in the stillness of my heart
Inside, I was bleeding from the piercing of love's darts

I'd pushed aside any chance
to resuscitate butterfly emotions
Devastated from reckless abandonment...and so I sank
slooowly into sorrow's ocean

Then without notice, you appeared
to cloak me with your love
Somehow you knew what my weeping heart was in need of

I'm so sorry, but I don't want to believe in love yet again
Only to be re-drowned from its downpour of hurting rain

Besides, how do you propose to bring me
into the marvel of your light?
By mounting me upon wings of
chivalry my Black Knight?

Rolling out the red carpet
escorting my every step
I want desperately to fall into you, but I must
guard this pulsation inside my chest

Yet, your love pressed in and cautiously I
presented you with the chance
To shower me with romance
despite raging circumstances

So, please promise me that if
I confess my love you'll not flee
Leaving me to sink upon a lover's Titanic
with no heart and no key

"Slavery takes hold of few, but many take hold of slavery."

-Seneca

Subjugation

Intertwined together, separated, then none
Sometimes I feel like the remainder of one

A pair that doesn't match; loneliness untold
Deciding to stay even though my soul is sold

Abandoned in the monotony of regular routines
Fading every day, the figure I once seen

Out of touch with reality is how I feel
Crying out for true love, a place where I can heal

Melanie E. Williams

Man's inhumanity to man makes
countless thousands mourn."

-Robert Burns

What He Gets At Night

Oh say that you see in the morning's early light
The slave master leaves when it's no longer night

Back to the 'Big House' where everything's pure
<u>every</u> thing is so pure
Come nightfall he'll return
this is for sure

He doesn't stay you know,
because the shacks simply lack
Nevertheless, he goes because
black skins draw him back

Seldom does he touch 'Missy' because...well...
she's too white
And what he craves most...
he gets at night... with no fight

Soon the result of master's deeds can be seen
A child is born
The color?
Coffee with cream

The Mrs. feels hurt, and the slave
is so glad they're through
but the child is not accepted
despite its heritage and hue

Master is pleased and lists his property with a smile
And so it goes in the life of a slave child...

"There is always something ridiculous about the emotions of people whom one has ceased to love."

-Oscar Wilde

Woman's Sorrow Part One

...There in the shadows; shoulders slumped and head bowed
Stood a woman within a woman that no longer felt proud
As she sighed to herself shaking her head to and fro
Choking with the reality that a lover has let go

Struggling to stand tall though her knees were very weak
As he watched her in silence; silence was
all they could speak
Because she was inebriated from bottled
rejection and spoiled love
Her desire was to give him her love in spite of

And to cover the incision of a friend's bleeding heart
Because he understood the pain when
love tears your heart apart
So, as they stood there she clutched him;
the cloth to cover her wound
Alone in the shadow's wavered two lonely souls in tune

Melanie E. Williams

Lessons Learned

Before the Beginning
Don't Speak
Evaporated
First, Touch Me There
Had It. Lost It.
Lessons
Love Fog
Question for Destiny
Rearview
Rhythmic Love
Standin' Alone
Taking Aim
Unchained
Wanting It Back
Woman's Sorrow Part Two

"We are but as the instrument of Heaven. Our work is not design, but destiny."

-Lord Lytton

Before the Beginning

Long ago, before you took your first steps
A plan was put together in heaven that was quietly kept
The years rolled along and with them you grew humble and wise
And then the day came that with my touch, you opened your eyes

Before you stood your blessing; no, it was no curse
So, believe me when I say you are each other's first
Your first time being overjoyed to a point you couldn't speak
Yes, at first glance you smiled big but your knees were so weak

You questioned yourselves and even questioned me. Is this for real?
Then my voice said unto thee, "I need you two to be very still."
And while you are standing, please be firm
There's going to be some things that will make you squirm

You may want to yield; not go another mile
But if you can stand to be blessed, it will come in a while
"What will come?" You both asked...Be patient and you'll know
That what I've blessed you with will forever grow and grow

Now, the roads may sometimes be rocky, but you two are strong
And if you refuse to bow down, then there's no way you'll go wrong
Some people may try to smite; others will be glad to see
That the souls I've put together are blessed by me

The enemy will even try to make you believe
That what was created wasn't Heavenly conceived
And he will attack at each and every chance he gets
But, remember to stand firm because I'm molding you and yet...

...For being steadfast, my awesome blessing for the each of you
Is really quiet beautiful... You see, my gift is you two...

Melanie E. Williams

"I know nothing swifter in life
than the voice of rumor."

-Plautus

Don't Speak

Listening to rumors so out of control
Useless facts constantly invading my soul

Trying to resist the temptation to hear?
Whispers of laughter?
A slander?
A sneer?

Where it begins, it simply does not end
A continuous cycle of words that offend

Feeling the urge to make a reputation weak?
Do your spirit a favor... and don't speak

Everyone's talking about the why and where
In walks the subject
shhh...
lips mute
eyes stare

Looking for fragmented information to spread
People repeating what "he said" and "she said"

It's more than enough to make a person want to scream
Daily participation in vicious blaspheme

No longer the urge to defile or critique
So I'm refusing to listen... and I will not speak!

"When a man has once loved a woman, he will do anything
for her except continue to love her."

-Oscar Wilde

Evaporated

By the time that you believe my love for you was strong
It will be too late...I will have journeyed on

When you're reflecting upon tranquility gracing my face
I'll be gallivanting through winds with no trace

So sad you cast away this beautiful amour
An exquisite woman that adored you four-score

Now you seek to find me once again
You've realized to be without me made you insane

But I'm gone away with a memory you beseech
My love has forever vanished... it's no longer in reach

Melanie E. Williams

"You have to penetrate a woman's defenses. Getting into her head is a prerequisite to getting into her body."

-Bob Guccione

First, Touch Me There

So you ask me how I want it
Well...let me tell you this
I want you to permeate my life
incite emotion for every crevice

Now, once you've excited the intellect of my mind
Like... pantomime ways
to make my heart
your lifeline

Then, we can proceed
to consummating in non-traditional ways
Like making love on counter tops
in Parisian cafes

Or devouring strawberries from our bodies
in the heat of St.Croix
And if you desire my sweet,
inside the Wooden Horse of Troy

See...my list could go on
about the sensual things we could do
But, if you can't touch me there
I'd have to bid you adieu

Return to me not until you
can feed me more than a line
Because you can't make love to my body, baby
until you have first, made love to my mind

"Twenty years a child; twenty years running wild; twenty years
a mature man --and after that, praying."

-Irish Proverb

Had It. Lost It.

I know things can't remain the same
Right now I'm talking about the sum of my frame

I sure miss my youth
Didn't know what I had back then to tell you the truth

Today, I was so glad I didn't order ice cream
Foods like that make me scream in my favorite jeans

Time has changed me from a raving beauty
To barely having time to finish daily duties

Between carpooling, ball games, making lunches
and loading backpacks
I'm still trying to figure out where
the hell my sanity's at!

People have told me that some things fly with time
They forgot to mention so does your patience and your mind

Oh well...that's the way it goes

Melanie E. Williams

"In every man there is something wherein I may learn of him,
and in that I am his pupil."

-Ralph Waldo Emerson

Lessons

Every now and then I stumble upon a sappy soul that has a
taunted agenda; to tear down my dream, rain upon my parade
or say and do everything to make me their slave.

So, I snap open my umbrella, pack plenty of mortar and bricks
so I can build a wall to protect me from
their treacherous bags of tricks.

People like that are the reason I keep a pad and a pen
To take many notes and then... I'm going to strive never to be
like them.

"I am the love that dare not speak its name."

-Alfred Douglas

Love Fog

Sometimes it's like passion when it's fresh and new
It blocks ones vision by keeping reality from full view

It's annoying, misleading and will remove the light
Leaves people fondling, guessing, and blind
with perfect sight

With deception, it urges one to move closer within
Disobey the sixth sense and allow it to win

Somehow it cataracts the eyes, breaking
down the weak and strong
Then suddenly it disappears
and the love fog moves on

Melanie E. Williams

"No friendship, no love can cross the path of our destiny
without leaving some mark on it forever."

-Francois Muriac

Question for Destiny

Something about you is different and sweet in
a mellow kind of way
You're an anomaly of a man and I hope you don't mind if I say
I think you are strong and striking; easy on my eyes
Aside from the physical, mentally you're my type

You propel me to think a bit deeper than I do
Baby, I need to bear caution because I
could really get into you
Oh man, grey skies are fleeting whenever
your voice is in my ear
Mmmm, if only I could have you nearer to make
the sounds I love to hear

We could choreograph our own rain dance
Making love under sun's shine at every chance
And with you sucking on me like freshly plucked fruit
I know you're feelin' me as much as I'm feelin' you

But jolly ole fate has mixed up our dates
Or did it? Is this the right time? The right place?
Is our destiny this moment? I think so.
How else would our story go?

But, I said all of that my sweet; only to say this
I dig the way my mind you caress with such finesse
And I hope you feel that 'something' people sometimes do
When they know something is comfortable, different, and
new...

"The beauty of the past is that it is the past.
The beauty of the now is to know it.
The beauty of the future is to see where one is going."

-Unknown

Rearview

Whatever he desired, I freely gave
See...my fixation to a lover converted me into his slave

Bound by his touch and meaningless words
So, I settled into a relationship where love was deferred

As I waited in silence for him to free my mind
I exchanged my 'self' for actions unkind

Lowered my being only for his embrace
not knowing I was only a woman with no face

He was tied to a past that presently caused pain and
down to my knees I stayed to receive his hurting rain

I sought his acceptance, because I adored him so
Knowing that his love for me would never overflow

Because imprisoned was he and imprisoned was I
Yet, our only solace was found in a little white lie

Soon my mind decided what my heart declared 'no can do'
and I moved forward with my life, leaving him in the rearview

Melanie E. Williams

"Nothing is to come, and nothing past;
But an eternal now does always last."

-Abraham Cowley

Rhythmic Love

Tick to the rhythm of our love then tock
Keep the tempo of my pulse and this
passion will never stop

Step in time to the artful dance to my soul
Sway to the beat of my spirit
and this adoration shall never age old

Like hands synchronized in motion
upon the face of a clock
Ticking to the rhythm of our song
means our love hasn't stopped

"Conceit is a queer disease--it makes everyone sick
except the person who has it."

-Unknown

Standin' Alone

I met a man before who thought he was the shh_t!
All he talked about was his women, his money, and his car
What he had in his house, how much he'd traveled, how far

Pockets all thin...chest all swoll
Knew he was the shh_t! without ever being told

You know... when I think about this man...
he really was shh_t!
He wasn't all that...he never was it

He never produced fruit from any kind of tree
He was busy milkin' women for what he got scot-free

Too busy frontin' for others without
thinkin' about his back
And wearin' feigned faces 'cause his personality lacked

Spent most of his time conjuring plans to deceive women
Not caring how they felt while
he continuously mistreated them

Because he was the man, he was supposed to do that
He was supposed to keep takin' without ever givin' back

He was supposed to be catered to and treated like a king
Since women's sole design was to pacify his longings

Yeah...he thought he was golden
and he thought he was it
But in the end you stand alone my man
when you think you're the shh_t!

Melanie E. Williams

"A man's reach should exceed his grasp, or what's heaven for?"

-Robert Browning

Taking Aim

I'm gonna keep holding on because I have no choice
It's either do or die and I'm not ready to give up my ghost

Got a lot of earth to tread, dreams to bring to fruition,
people to love and for them to love me back. I'm not tryin' to
boast

As a woman and not a girl feigning maturity, but a queen
I'm determined to keep a grip on my life; even if sometimes
I step outside the line

My focus is like a sharpshooter taking aim. The mark through
my scope is on life all the time

"The secret of happiness is freedom,
and the secret of freedom, courage."

-Thucydides

Unchained

Listen up!

I want everyone to know that I courageously proclaim!
My freedom from the black that blued
because...I...am... unchained!

From strong hands that was supposed to lift
me through life's flames
But instead used my body as its aim
and so frail I became

The nights I cried in silence
my mind bound and gagged
Cause I couldn't break away
from a hold that was ironclad

As I look back now,
I see that situation was pretty sad
How I allowed him to convince me
his pitiful love was all I really had

When in actuality,
I had so so much more than that
More than a body for him
to beat upon for this and that

I had a spark!
A glimmer of hope!
A will to remain!
And I opened it up to flourish
with the keys that made me unchained!

Melanie E. Williams

"Remorse begets reform"

-William Cowper

Wanting It Back

When you learned that I had strong feelings for you
Break up was your response; you was too through

So, I swallowed my pride and drank gallons of pain
I knew this familiar story; the face was
different but the man was the same

In time I could proceed with life,
and I met someone so kind

Funny how you then decided to
turn back the hands of time

Now you want me back because I found someone true
Didn't you tell me before that we were through!?

Oh ok...now suddenly you have a change of heart;
Now, I'm all that!
Just two months ago you felt you couldn't go back!

Everything is cool. Let's just stick
with your first decision

You moved on with your life. And as for me?? Oh yeah,
well...I'm still livin'

"Resolve to be thyself: and know, that he
who finds himself, loses his misery."

-Matthew Arnold

Woman's Sorrow Part Two

Yes, it was once upon a time I searched for
a remedy to cure my pain
From the disappointment of a love gone
wrong and consequently made me insane
What I needed was the anecdote to return me to a place
In time when all was bright before
I fell from my love's grace

I was grasping at straws, sipping fad potions,
and slowly fading each day
"How could I let someone do this to me?"
Was the question I replayed
Then, in a different kind of
darkness a voice said unto me
Whispering with calm resolve that
I had already been freed

And that no one held me in bondage
because I ever possess the key
To unlock the chains that bind in love
When I am not free to be me
That alone made my spirit overflow with life
As I lay me down to sleep that night
I believed I would be alright

After the gloaming, the warmth of the sun
Kissed and blessed my face
And restored to me the woman within the woman
Returning to embrace love's grace
But, this time around I was not holding him;
the lover with emotions outdated
Instead, I was holding me once more…a woman
Forever celebrated

Melanie E. Williams

Gratitude and Victory

Affirmations to the Woman in the Mirror
Angel Friend
As If I Were a Queen
Creating in Rain
Deck
Go Ahead
Grape Cape
Him
Let Me Peel This Off
Lost
My Course of Time
Overflowin'
Senses of Love
Shades in My Mind
Strong
Summer of My Season
Think Only This of Me
While You Slept

"This above all: To thine self be true,
and it must follow, as the night the day, thou
canst not then be false to any man."

-Shakespeare

Affirmations to the Woman in the Mirror

Isn't it odd how we can avow to others with
conviction that which we do not give to ourselves?
Promises made, time spent,
full devotion showered upon those we meet,
and things purchased with ink portraits
of people from years past?

I am choosing a new affirmation; to boldly
proclaim an unfathomable truth
I love you!
To the reflection in my eyes
An image of self
It is Y.O.U that I adore!

The preciousness in your spirit
words you sweetly sing
the warmth in your caress
and the movement of your frame
I am enchanted with your being
Yes
Y.O.U!

Your existence defies all reasoning because
the reach of your presence knows no bounds
you are my sea to shining sea
infinite rays of light
my slow moving river
green succulent mountains
my mysterious galaxy aglow with billions
of incandescent symbols of my love
It is Y.O.U I adore!

Melanie E. Williams

"Forsake not an old friend; for the new is not comparable to him. A new friend is as new wine when it is old. Thou shalt drink it with pleasure."

-Bible

Angel Friend

You entered my life
ever to protect me from the pain
You spread your wings around me graciously
to shield me from the rain
Amazingly, I witnessed this friendship unfold
Always standing by my side to comfort my soul

Encouraged me to be
all that I was destined
Showered my existence with wisdom
angel friend
You held my hand tight as
our relationship budded, blossomed,
then finally took flight

Separate or together until Eternity's end
You'll forever have my heart,
my love, angel friend
Never forget that our time
was truly well spent
Yes, an angel friend like you
is a spirit heaven sent

Thank you for being someone
upon whom I could depend
You've been there for me from
beginning to end
And so, I'll take hold of my memories
and suspend them in time
Forever will I love you
my haloed angel friend of mine

"He who is plenteously provided for from within,
needs but little from without."

-Johann Wolfgang Von Goethe

As If I Were a Queen

Did you know that I was a Queen?
Not solely because I possess material things
But because I walk with freedom hand and hand
That's more than some can say who live in foreign lands

Before, I never saw myself as royalty; I didn't realize...
I am a Queen! I can speak without fear inside my eyes!
I can march on capitols and express my views
Or even discuss politics in a circle of many or few

Even more than that, I can pursue my dreams
I bathe in porcelain tubs and not rivers or streams
My religion I can practice morning noon or night
My country won't murder me for my
beliefs in the brazen light

And I can generate more income than
presidents on distant soil
My food is purchased in clean markets;
the earth I don't have to toil

To many, I live like a Queen
I represent a life they have never seen
A moment of time they wish they could capture
With family and friends resounding in peaceful laughter

From here on out, I will think twice
Of people near or far whose struggle is life
Who look upon me as if I were a Queen
In a land of plenty... where no one must glean

Melanie E. Williams

"No pain, no palm; no thorns, no throne;
no gall, no glory; no cross, no crown."

-William Penn

Creating In Rain

You've helped me to create at a time like this
Memories now hurt; they're no longer of bliss

Offensive words that have caused me pain
But, I'm creating now in a world of rain

No more moments of love and peace
The agony I feel never seems to cease

I'm creating now as you take away your touch
Oh, how I wanted you soooo much

Yet, slowly the wheels of creativity rotate
Around a love that wasn't designed by fate

Locked in a world that pulls my heart reins
Forges me to create in a world of pain

"Peace is liberty in tranquility."

-Cicero

Deck

Here I sit on an island where no man lives alone
Embracing luxury in a peace I've captured as my own

Watching the sun set below arms of greenery
I whisper to myself, "This is what I've dreamt for me."

Here, away from the rituals of daily life
I'm enchanted by the river, a gentle breeze
Mmmmmm... my soul's so satisfied

They say no man's an island;
that no one stands alone
But here in intimate surroundings
I feel the comforts of home

Melanie E. Williams

"How sweet it is to love, and to be dissolved,
and as it were to bathe myself in thy love."

-Thomas Kempis

Go Ahead

Continue to caress my body
like love kneading love
Gaze into my eyes
seek the beauty and passion within
Find me

Continue with melodious tales of laughter
Make the radiance of my smile
permanently banish darkness
Amuse me

Continue to bring me
to a place of pleasure
that keeps me inebriated
Resuscitate me
then take me again, higher and higher
Seduce me

Continue understanding my composition
Listen to my symphony
move to the rhythm of my life
Love me

"If not for her, all would have been lost."

-Melanie E. Williams

Grape Cape

Unable to leap from buildings to make a great escape
Because she was destined to form souls into the number of
eight

So, she walked rugged mile after mile
through snow and torrential rain
Using only her grape cape to shield her from pain

Blocking from every angle; possessors of woe
the grape-caped woman with the figure of eight souls

Within a down pour a sweat, toil and tears
The tattered drapery protected her year after year

Then one still day, she loosed its bow
Time had come to let the grape cape go

Into a visible case she hung it next to a letter
Stating her dreams must be delayed because she
was the figure eight soul's mother

Tired and worn from a long life journey
She reclined and reflected upon her pre-appointed duty

She thought and she thought and then whispered with a
smile, "The cape and souls of eight, has made it all
worthwhile."

Melanie E. Williams

"If the sea were ink for the words of my Lord, the sea would be
spent before the Words of my lord are spent."

-Qur'an

Him

For the pure, clean water I drink each day
And the warmth of the sun that embraces my face

For the breeze that flows through on a hot summer night
As I watch my beautiful son while wrapped in moonlight

For the ability to move with no physical pain
Yes, I understand with each day a blessing I've gained

You don't have to smile upon my life with such ease
I know that you could turn the other way if you pleased

And smile upon another and to bless them so much
But I would wither and die if I couldn't feel your touch

Or if you looked upon me with an expression so sad
I'd grip the cup of woe until my final days passed

So, this is why I thank you; for all your sweet grace
By your finger, you've engraved my life with your trace

I thank you
I love you for all that you do
My Redeemer
My Friend
My God, you are true

"Above the clouds with its shadow is the star with its light.
Above all things reverence thyself."

-Pythagoras

Let Me Peel This Off

I've never known a love like this before
One that keeps my eyes lowered to the floor

Haunts me in the thick of night and makes my heart sweat
A love that induces every ounce of my soul with regret

Sends me on a hunt for new love
and a new brand of affection
Only to find it with a man gift-wrapping rejection

I have never known a love that made me feel used
A sick sense of emotion showered solely on the abused

The type of love that robs me of my humanity
Makes me fail to remember it is OK to love me

Never known this kind of love until I met you
Never want to experience it again
that is why we are through

Melanie E. Williams

"Loyalty binds me."

-Motto

Lost

My precious lover, will you promise to search for me
When we are separated by the vastness of seas?

Quest far and wide for the one you adore?
My beloved, come for the one who loves you more

Promise to conquer the strength of
a mountain rugged and wide
Look for me gentle lover...promise me you will try

Unfold your wings across the skies of devotion, my sweet
Sail the earth for a love that penetrates your core deep

Will you travel the distance of earth's span?
To repossess the one that weeps for the
touch of your hands?

I'll wait for you dear lover until eternity's end
You're the one that completes my life time and again

"That it will never come again
is what makes life so sweet."

-Emily Dickinson

My Course of Time

All I have is this moment
the one suspended in time
To live out a dream or lend a hand
to humanity when humanity's unkind

All I have is this moment
to show compassion and love
Inhale all the richness of life by
spreading my wings like a dove

All I have is this moment
to turn my life into a song
Create melodies with harmony
that compels the weak to be strong

All I really have now
is this one moment to live
To partake in the beauty of God
and so my life I give

Melanie E. Williams

"Chameleons feed on light and air
Poets' food is love and fame."

-Percy Bysshe Shelley

Overflowin'

You've got my creativity flowin'
Like rivers spilling into oceans

Like sand trickling to the bottom of an hourglass
Or spicy energized sex that lasts and lasts and lasts

My mind is open like a virgin on her very first night
This creativity is fluid...yet...tight

My thoughts are tickin' like the hands on a clock
When I'm grippin' my pen filled with verse, I can't stop

Yeah, it was you that had me creating in rain
About an experience filled with your joy and my pain

But that's ok 'cause now I am overflowin'
Like rivers plunging and crashing deeply into oceans

"We are all instruments endowed with feeling and memory.
Our senses are so many strings that
are struck by surrounding objects and
that also frequently strike themselves."

-Denis Diderot

Senses of Love

Love smells like freshly plucked flowers
And perfume that skin devours
Fresh baked pies from warm ovens
Scented bodies prepared for close huggin'

Love tastes like a velvety skinned peach
Refreshing peppermints to keep life sweet
The freshest of ice cold milk and
French croissants that's softer than silk

Love sounds like cool whispers of wind
Or a beating heart when love enters in
Family and friends resounding with laughter
Now, that's the sound of love I'm after

Love looks like... the Madonna and Child
A face of innocence embraced by a smile
Glowing timbers on a wintry night
Contented souls when everything's right

Love feels like skin wrapped in mink
So warm to the follicles you're unable to think
It's the missing piece of an incomplete life
Enjoying the senses of love makes living so nice

Melanie E. Williams

"Of all God's gifts to the sighted man, color is holiest,
the most divine, the most solemn."

-John Ruskin

Shades in My Mind

Crimson, rose, bravery, bloodshed, blush, stop, fear, love,
apples, cherries, sunsets, rubies, strawberries, sports car,
fingernails, nuclear explosions, lips, flags...Red

Secrets, blindness, Africa, slim, smooth, shine, midnight,
unknowns, eight balls, movement, original, dominant,
wealth...Black

Sunrises, lemons, happiness, hope, encouragement, gold,
sunflowers, warmth, life, summer...Yellow

Nature, finances, broccoli, mints, oregano, new beginnings,
pine trees, grass, prosperity...Green

Royalty, power, boldness...Purple

Mangoes, oranges, rest, good book, tea, relaxing, fall...Orange

Untouched, pure, stainless, Ancient Rome, platinum...White

Boys, sky, jeans, suits, water, towels, peace, Heaven...Blue

"That which does not kill us makes us stronger."

-Friedrich Nietzche

Strong

That's what they say and what I've come to believe
Years ago it was so hard to conceive

But I am

Strong

Not just at times when I've been wronged
But to include those moments when it was time to move on

To pick up the pace through the course of the storm
Wasn't just about saving face

It was about assuring my heart was matched with my mind
Fighting subtle demons in a world so sublime

Yeah, that's what they tell and I've come to believe
I. Am. Strong.

Melanie E. Williams

"One must know oneself. If this does not serve to discover
truth, it at least serves as a rule of life
and there is nothing better."

-Blaise Pascal

Summer of My Season

Faced with confidence I have
achieved change by striving
with a newfound freedom, leaves me
in the sun of my season

I am a butterfly, yet internally ever
blossoming like the beauty of a rose
The clarity of my prime has guided
me to sanity's reason

Never did I imagine the vanes of
direction leading me to the
comforts of my soul
I pray such surety doesn't
lead me to unearthly treason

And so, I shall grasp the excitement of the sun
Fly like eagles under the winds of spring
Aspiring never to betray humanity nor self
as I embrace my life in the summer of my season

"Love must be as much a light,
as it is a flame."

-Henry David Thoreau

Think Only This of Me

As far as the ocean is from the sky
Forever I will hold you
my love for you shall never die

From this life unto the next
think only this of me...
I hope the beauty in my spirit
is all you'll ever see

The softness of my touch
and security of my arms
The grace within my smile
the splendor of my charm

Contemplate this forever more
Because it is you I simply adore

Think only this...
when you remember
the glow within me
I am thinking of you
from now until eternity

Melanie E. Williams

"The largest barrier to success is removing the mattress from one's back in the morning."

-Source Unknown

While You Slept

While you were sleeping, I was barely age three
But there I stood with a mic in front of me

Singing melodies everyone thought so absolute
My audience was small; there was just a few

People always told me, I'd someday shine bright
So, while you were sleeping, I worked towards my guiding light

It seemed dim at times; when the battle felt old
Still, I knew that I needed to settle my soul

With reassuring thoughts about while you decided to sleep
My dream would finally break free through miniature leaps

And bound to a place where I now stand
Not in front of a few, but millions of fans

Between the Motion and the Act

People You Know

Desperados
Exception
Faces of Feign
Forgery
Gold Digger
I Think I Know You
Inamorata
Lese' Maj'esty
Lines
Me
Mr. Big Man
Name That Addiction
Us

Melanie E. Williams

"At the beginning and end of love, the two lovers
are embarrassed to find themselves alone."

-La Bruyere

Desperados

Lovers so lonely reaching
far into the night
Struggling to touch someone who'll
make their bodies take flight

Sad, sweet paramours embracing
the stars with the moon
Quietly moving gracelessly
to an unrehearsed tune

Gripping the symbol of passion
and forsaking all they know
Enveloping fireplace fantasies
whilst the embers project its glow

Two dispirited, looonely lovers
exhausted by the dream
are unnerved by a message
in this play's final scene

Parting ways is difficult
for the lovers still in strife
If only they explored with passion
could they find a love so right

"If you are pained by external things, it is not they that disturb you, but your own judgment of them. And it is in your power to wipe out that judgment now."

-Marucs Aurelius

Exception?

Just because your skin is pallid
doesn't mean you don't lie
Just because your eyes are slanted
doesn't mean you don't cry

Just because your skin is cerise
doesn't mean you will kill
And just because you are bronze
doesn't mean you will steal

Just because you don't belong
doesn't make you an outcast
Just because you are succeeding
doesn't mean that it will last

Just because you are stealing
doesn't mean you can't get caught
And just because you are buying
doesn't mean it can be bought

Melanie E. Williams

"I detest that man who hides one thing in the depth
of his heart and speaks forth another."

-Homer

Faces of Feign

Looking on the surface never reveals the soul
Casual conversations shed no light
on stories untold

Locked away in a gorge where dark secrets reside
But the passage of time uncovers what
the heart tries to hide

The mouth eventually yields
all the poison held within
The world is now made aware of the secret sin

The message is brought forth
and for you, that person's no longer the same
This time around, you see the faces of feign

"No one should part with their individuality
and become that of another."

-William Channing

Forgery

Try hard if you can but so many things
about me you cannot fake
no way to carbon copy my intelligence,
style, spirit, and grace

The outer me can be purchased
the clothes, the shoes, the dress
But, the inner me shall never be sold
this... I know you detest

With infinity, you could never recreate me
I stand alone
It's sickening to think
you do not have an image to call your own

There is no competition if you can believe this to be true
Allow me to be me and define yourself for you

Class cannot be copied
It's cultivated over time and then...
A masterpiece is created
for the person possessing it within

So, buy the clothes I like
purchase the perfumes I use
In the meantime... I'm forever a winner
while you are confused about you

The world can tell the difference
because I am true to me
You're not being original
and that's plain to see

Melanie E. Williams

"The poor man's budget is full of schemes."

-Proverb

Gold Digger

Don't have skills to call
her own so go figure

Picks her targets by the quality of his shoes
After sexin' him right
he's completely subdued

He's satisfied cause she satisfies
though money's her aim
He's too busy in board meetings
to recognize her game

She stays in the shops
buying the expensive and unique
Her man banks six digits
so her lifestyle's of quality

Always discussing that and this
But without that man
she has no window
for the pot she's pissed

Gold digger
Her man lassoes six
digits so go figure

"Now I believe I can hear the philosophers protesting that it can only be misery to live in folly, illusion, deception and ignorance, but it isn't—it's human."

-Desiderius Erasmus

I Think I Know You

For a cheap thrill she exchanged modest joy for moderate pain
Neglected all the players for that quick-fix dosage to her veins

Forgot altogether what she learned; to walk the streets at night
Provided dark services for those in dark suits and crisp shirts of white

Wearing the latest in fashion... up and down the cat walk
Her throat's so raw from the finger, she can barely talk

Trashed the newborn problem she chose to ignore
Someone found him...but she has no feelings for the one she just bore

The magazine says she is supposed to look just like her
So, under the knife she goes to change her face and to the salon to change her hair

People laugh when she walks away with a bag of burgers in each hand
They don't care that it's been years since she's been in average-sized pants

In her teenage years, she dyes her hair of different shades
And to secretly vent tamed emotions, she turns to the razor blade

We know these women, everyday we pass them by
Yet silently, their souls weep enough to create tides

Melanie E. Williams

"There is something to me very softening in the presence
of a woman, some strange influence...which I cannot
at all account for..."

-Lord Byron

Inamorata

She makes men stare with hunger in their eyes
Surveying her delights is where
their thoughts lie

Without caution they ignite bravery within
to ask her for meetings of a love involving skin

Amazed to see how some at their climax...fall
for the pleasures of her warmth, they exchange it all

Never realized the strength in what she had
being a precious inamorata with a 'grip' that's ironclad

"Those who are faithful know only the trivial side of love;
it is the faithless that know love's tragedies."

-Oscar Wilde

Lese' Maj'esty

In the dark she makes excuses
because she wants to break away
He tells his wife he needs fresh air
then makes his way to where 'she' waits

They proceed to that place so familiar
where he does those special things
while she holds him close to her breasts
then sends him home quivering

In route, he practices the lies
to his wife he must calmly tell
And she never reveals her secret
about the one who has her under a spell

He thinks he is cool
Playing his wife for a fool
While the other's just a tool
But he will eventually get schooled

She checks her cell because
he calls her each day
to meet at 'the spot'
so they can go where they lay

Finally, their lies can no longer
be used so they pack them away
The lovers are now ostracized
for lese' maj'esty

Melanie E. Williams

"Oh what a tangled web we weave,
when first we practice to deceive!"

-Sir Walter Scott

Lines

Ever had a man to feed you an antiquated line?
And you can tell the way he delivered it
it worked every time?

Like..."What's a lovely woman like you doing here?"
Or how about..."Come here baby
so I can whisper somethin' in your ear."

"Heyyy! Don't I know you from somewhere?
Listen...(he says while looking around)
let's get out of here
I'll take you anywhere
We can ride allll night
I don't care."

"Ummm girl, your perfume smells so sweet!"
And let's not forget...
"Why don't you come to my place
so I can cook you somethin' to eat."

"Look at you...pretty hair,
nice skin, thick hips...
I bet you can really kisss
with those sssweet, sssoft lipsss."

It's a different face
but the lines are the same
A similar man...
but with a different name

Runnin' game...runnin' game

"She walks in beauty, like the night of cloudless
climbs and starry skies; And all that's best of
dark and bright met in her aspect in her eyes."

-Lord Byron

Me

By definition it means Black
its origin... is Greek
Some try to discover the inscrutable
because I am unique

One potent experience will reveal
a beauty inspiring the soul
C'mere...take a quick glance and see
what others desire to hold and behold

Filled with femininity
to me a joy and never a curse
Graced with elegance and a pen
filled with poetic verse

Soft, honey-colored skin
accented by a smile so serene
And an enchanting face encasing eyes
the color of Paris-green

A name that means dark, but for me
I'm a Star shining bright
Peer into my life and experience
life filled with light

Melanie E. Williams

"He that is proud eats up himself."

-Shakespeare

Mr. Big Man

Look at Mr. Big Man with the new Italian suit
Italian shoes, attaché case and an expensive car to boot

A good job, expensive home, and caviar is what he prefers
Forgotten whom he was; just putting on airs

Miles away from home, the Big Man is living the life
Did I also fail to mention he has a very lovely wife?

The Big Man knew he was just a little man
before landing 'the job'
Making it from paycheck to paycheck
and livin' like a slob

Try telling this to him and he will categorically deny
that he ever lived like a pauper and he never had a wife

He never robbed Peter to try to pay Paul
He never went hungry 'cause he's always had it all

He dared not mingle with commoners
because that's simply not his taste
He's always been very classy
living each day with style and grace

Take a look at Mr. Big Man with all his material things
Not one item can bring him the happiness he's missing

Years from now Mr. Big Man will be just a man
No expensive shoes on his feet, no attaché case in hand

When the spotlight has faded and 'the life' has passed away
I wonder what this man will do and what he'll have to say?

"The chains of habit are generally too small to be felt
until they are too strong to be broken."

-Samuel Johnson

Name That Addiction

One man loves the bottle, the other chooses the pipe
One hugs the plate, while some grip the knife

She digs deep into her wallet
he replays the X-rated tape
She gossips with many
he hates another ones race

The casino lures him there, the streets call her name
It doesn't matter how you dress it
all addictions are the same

Her hands she can't keep clean
A remote supports his frame
She's checked the locks 10 times already
He's hustling for the game

This one longs for children, the other one cannot trust
That one enjoys falsehood, for some... stealing is a must

Call it what you want
Dress it as you choose
Denying your addictions
Means someone has to lose

Picking pockets, abusive hands
Serial murderers, deceptive plans

Paint it any color
Hide it if you choose
Denying your addictions
Means someday you will lose

Melanie E. Williams

"Personal beauty is a greater recommendation than any letter
of reference."

-Aristotle

Us

Bella donne with a smile so sweet casts
her eyes to a star so bright...
Saturn on a clear summer's night

Feathery locks in the Senegalese Twists
Admiring bella donne isn't a moment I'd miss

Sometimes circumstances washes away peace upon her face
Look at bella donne handle life as if time didn't matter
And neither did pace

Funny how her eyes changes color from that
of the Adriatic Sea
to bursting colors of spring to the color of coffee

Bella donne
My beauty
My grace
Every woman I love
From every place I've graced

Something to Relate To

Abyss of Love
All Caught Up
Buried
Captured
Good Love
He's Fixed
Inked Emotions
Just a Piece
My Noble Man
My Time
Peep This...Twice
Rainbows
Reminisce This
Repeat That
Rotations
Swerve
This Is Getting Old
Winter Sensation
You Promise

Melanie E. Williams

"In their first passion, women love their lovers;
in all the others, they love love."

-La Rochefouccauld

Abyss of Love

The taste of your sweet lips ignites a fire filled
with desire longing never to be quenched. To be enraptured for
a moment with you stays in the forefront of my mind.
I am hungry for the softness of your breath; the sweet smell of
desire that never tires my soul.

Tender kisses soothe my face; wispy and light your lips land
and I am reminded of butterflies making delicate touches on
roses. I feel like a flower in bloom.

Your beautiful love makes way for me to break free; to extend
myself in ways I have never journeyed. Trembling from the
touch of your silky fingertips makes me want to fall into an
abyss of love only to be rescued by you.

I want to draw myself closer to the warmth of your skin and
the beating of your heart; fused forever in love never to part.

"For those who love, time is eternity."

-Unknown

All Caught Up

Here we are entangled in a moment
Just you and I
The mood is pink and all we can think about
is how much we love each other
faults and fun

When I look at you
the only thing I can comprehend
is that you are the most intriguing person
God has ever formed

Everything about you is so right in my eyes
My mind's eye agrees
My memory has been searched
and it is conclusive

No one I have ever loved before
can hold a candle to the one
I am so deeply in love with now
Shhhh...
Can you hear it?
The wind is playing our song!

Let's dance!
And when we are finished dancing
let's just lie in a field of daisies
and listen to our hearts
beat against the earth
then drift off into enchanted dreams

Entangled...

Melanie E. Williams

"People who die are not buried in a field,
they are buried in the heart."

-Anonymous

Buried

Absorbed within my heart
a past lover is buried so deep
I entombed him there
because tender memories make me weep

My eyes overflow when I think about his touch
or the times we made love sparingly...yet much

Should I reflect upon the tenderness
of each passionate kiss
Out comes a shovel to exhume the love I reminisce

I miss him more as the earth revolves around the sun
But, I hesitate to let this man know
he's my special someone

So sorry, I must plant my feelings where
former attachments lie
to permanently bury you inside my heart
dear lover...goodbye

"It is an art to recollect."

-Kierkegaard

Captured

I don't want to exhale because then I'd
move into another interval of time
I want to freeze-frame our love
and implant it in my mind

There, I could feel your touch
and the gentleness of your hands
Savor the warmth of your mouth
and where each tender kiss lands

Enjoy the look of desire
that lovingly fills your eyes
As you stroke my spirit while
you slowly penetrate my life

I don't want to breathe
I just want to abide in your strong arms
Taste the scent of your skin and
revel in the splendor of your charm

I refuse to release this moment
In my mind is where it will stay
Until we love again my love
this moment I will replay

Melanie E. Williams

"She who has never loved has never lived."

-John Gay

Good Love

I want a really, really good love
the kind that keeps me high
I crave the kind of love
that longs to keep you nigh

Yes, give it to me
the essence that makes me quake
Increases my pulse
makes me quiver
makes me shake

I'm searching for some love
that lasts throughout the day
Propels me to touch your picture
when you're far far away

Passionate
fulfilling
committed
secure
and warm

I want a really, really good love
the kind that makes me cry
The kind that holds it all together
and one that never dies

"He who is in love is wise and is becoming wiser. Sees newly every time he looks at the object beloved, drawing from it with his eyes and his mind whose virtues which it possesses."

-Ralph Waldo Emerson

He's Fixed

Honey, with your touch the sol shines bright
And you put the glow in fireflies
on a clear summer's night
Turquoise skies pour out bows from rain
My life once crazy... has now been made sane

Did you know the earth no longer quakes?
And at night Honey, I pray to the Lord my love you'll take?
Through your touch my universe is peacefully still
Plus, I'm always in good health with
you around Honey, I'm never ill

Butterflies dance constantly on red roses in bloom
Because our souls are in tune even when
there's a full moon
And you tickle my fancy with humor so sweet
Speaking of sweet...that you are Honey
to the soles of your feet

The captivating feel of your body keeps me addicted
With your love Honey, I have been passionately afflicted
People ask if I'm in search of a cure
I think not!
You see...I crave the way my heart races
when you make me HOT! HOT!

And if someone offers love therapy, I'll refuse to join in
'Cause I need to have your love in my veins freely flowin'
I want to stay addicted to the clarity of life
To forever stare into your beautiful eyes
of jade and white

Melanie E. Williams

He's Fixed (cont'd)

I love being strung out on the creamy center of you
Honey, I'm like volcanic eruptions
when we are one instead of two

The ways you make me toss and turn each night in bed
Oh... to be withdrawn from you my love makes my
heart bleed dread---red

You're my morning star
My melody so serene
Consider me your king because
I've crowned you my queen

The sound of your voice
the shape of your hips
The intellect of your mind
your tender soft lips

You're the true beauty of life
and all that is sun-funny
I'm drawn to you like bees
because... you are my Honey

"Poetry is the spontaneous overflow of powerful feelings;
it takes its origin from emotion recollected in tranquility."

-William Wordsworth

Inked Emotions

The excitement I feel for you pours
from my heart to my pen
Creating poetic verses
dancing on paper 'til no end

With happiness one minute
the next flows bittersweet tears
as I record the intensity of my joys and fears

With the pulsation of my soul
I carefully hand pick each word
Inked emotions overflow onto pages
...confessions never heard

At no time have I been driven
to expose thoughts with such expression
It was the might of your love rushing in
unveiling the artist within

The passion I feel for you
flows from my heart to the pen
creating poetic verses for a love
I pray never ends

Melanie E. Williams

"I do not know whether I was then a man dreaming
I was a butterfly, or whether, I am now a butterfly
dreaming I am a man."

-Chuang-Tzu

Just a Piece

I feel butterflies dancing inside my heart
when you are around
Not because I'm smitten
but because I'm falling

I mean I've climbed Love's Mount Everest;
took one trembling leap from it's peak
and drif-ted
In slow motion towards your love

This is beautiful...

Who would have thought one human being
could propel another to let it all go
Yeah, I said it right the first time
I'm not infatuated
I am in love
With you

Catch me with your might
And even though I'm floating
it's gonna hit you hard like...like thrusts
Ok, Ok I'll stop here
But remember this...
I feel butterflies dancing inside my heart

"One can be a soldier without dying,
and a lover without sighing."

-Sir Edwin Arnold

My Noble Man

My long-time amour, newfound defender of our destiny
Do you realize there's no me without you
and no you without me?

You have been the circumference of my life;
my legs so I can stand
It's been a joy knowing you possess my hand
that showcases your band

The way you shampoo my tresses and massage my feet
Feed me delights delicious and coated
with your love so sweet

Breakfast in bed, movies, and bodies molded front to back
Always assuring your queen never lacks

My long-time amour
newfound defender of our destiny

Melanie E. Williams

"I would rather sit on a pumpkin, and have it all to myself, than be crowded on a velvet cushion."

-Henry David Thoreau

My Time

I feel like being alone today. I just want to shut off the world's ringer and go to a place of sheer quiet. I'm starved for some solitude. I really don't want to be bothered.

I don't want to be in a crowd nor with a lover. If you think I want to be held, you are wrong. Dead wrong. No thanks! See, I'm not craving a touch. I just want to go somewhere isolated, lock the door and vegetate for a while.

After that, I'm good. But for now, I just want to be alone.

"Everything has beauty, but not everyone sees it."

-Confucius

Peep This...Twice

So you wonder what it is
that makes their eyes double-glance?
This is only a guess... but... maybe
it's the thickness of my frame
or the scent of my hair fragranced

Or it could be the gentle way I smile
with a little 'come hither' in my wink
Maybe it's the hushed way I am
that simply propels them to think

About the calculations of my steps
or how deep my mind can go
What's my depth?
Wouldn't they loved to know
but my secret's quietly kept

So there's your answer
to one of the riddles of my life
Why they slow down their stride
to peep this once... then twice

Melanie E. Williams

"My heart leaps up when I behold
a rainbow in the sky."

-William Wordsworth

Rainbows

The mist has faded
and my vision is so clear
I see pass the sky's edge
to what is far and near

A unity of hues
bursting boldly through the sky
That symbol is unshaken
because its purpose provides

Look very closely and
its meaning you will see
how its colorful interpretation
creates a symphony

It can make you rich
in a very fulfilling way
Vivid rainbows
eternally stay

"Memory is the only paradise
from which we cannot be driven."

-Jean Paul

Reminisce This

Reminisce this my true lover... When the
stars twinkle it is symbolic of a quaint
incandescence that burns deep within my being

Forget not eyes staring with passion and soft
tender kisses that separates and unites us
Hands kneading flesh with delicate desire

Reminisce sighs of unbelief and drowning without
resistance into a world of unimaginable joy
Never forget quick glances that screamed
silent messages only you could decipher

Try never to release the moments our bodies
quivered from nothing less than ecstasy and
remembering how good it feels to feel alive

Reminisce this: Dreams of bodies in motion,
a smile so sweet, scents of us, savoring the taste
of lovemaking, supple breasts against a solid chest

Reminisce exploring every avenue that allowed our
bodies to make contact regardless of the act
Brief good-byes, calm conversations, a touch,
and precious memories of you and me
Reminisce...please...reminisce

Melanie E. Williams

"A man should consider how much he has
more than he wants."

-Joseph Addison

Repeat That??

Alright, now that you're finished with the yin and the yang
Break it down for me again
so I understand how we're the same??

See...what you're saying hasn't
really captured my attention
So allow me to explain a few things I failed to mention

Ok, generally speaking, I like a man
equally intelligent as me
One that doesn't crowd my space...
let's my spirit soar free

He feels a sense of pride
when I am dripped with the best
and knows that I am strong woman
so he doesn't try to oppress

And yes, I like a gentleman that's easy on my eyes
Not necessarily gorgeous to others
but to me he's a prize

The kind of man with a pair of hands—strong
And one I appreciate for sexin' me sweet, yet looong

A man that makes my hair follicles tingle
When our bodies and minds chemically intermingle

Because we are so into each other...
even the universe moves to our dance
Now, explain it me ooone laaast tiiime
how you're that kind of man??

"To every thing there is a season,
and a time to every purpose under the heaven."

-Bible

Rotations

All things change
Winter to spring

Caterpillars metamorphose

Life to death
Love to hate

Hate to love
Things below ascend above

Melanie E. Williams

"When in doubt, win the trick."

-Edmond Hoyle

Swerve

Oooh...I saw a man to-day
that snatched me back in time!
The tricks he performed with my body
did a number on my mind! Let. Me. Tell. You...

He had me seeing red
when all I wanted to see was white
But I couldn't leave him alone because...
he was the wine in my glass
and the crack in my pipe

I mean, I was addicted to what
he was throwin' around
The faster he built me up
it took him less time
to tear me down

But I was just too hooked to care
whether he treated me right or not
As long as I produced the honey
that kept his hands inside my pot

Don't laugh...
you've been there
everybody's played the fool
At one time or another
been someone else's tool

And that's ok because time has
made me all the more wise
Now, I just entertain him...
without entertaining his lies

"When you rationalize, you do just that.
You make rational lies."

-Unknown

This Is Getting Old

Stop feeding me words that you truly don't mean
Like... I'll always and forever be your beautiful queen

Stop complimenting my eyes and soft, silky hair
And telling me sh-- when you know you don't care

Stop telling other people that I am your lady
Cause when I ask you to chill, your answer's always maybe

Stop taking my heart through all this drama and woe
In one breath you're my friend, the next... my foe

Stop acting in ways that confuses the way I think
And believing your love is all I'll ever eat and drink

Don't look into my eyes and tell me big lies
Like you're on your way over, yet you rarely stop by

Or how my love puts you on a natural high
Yet you ignore how your callousness kills me inside

Do you realize how many times
you've already said goodbye?

Stop!

Start loving me in ways you know I deserve
Enjoy every inch of my feminine curves

Start, feeding me words that I want to hear
But make sure they're true and please be sincere

Melanie E. Williams

"Not snow, no, nor rain, nor beat, nor night keeps them from accomplishing their appointed courses with all speed."

-Herodotus

Winter Sensation

On the coldest of nights in a world unable to bloom frigidity is
melted by two souls in tune
With the frost suspended in trees
and solid ice upon the grass
Lovers whisper desires they pray will last
and last and last

"Nothing weighs lighter than a promise."

-German Proverb

You Promise?

Never say never no matter who you are
It wouldn't be wise to wage upon that star

Of a promise that binds the boldest of all bets
When in history has never ever been kept

It'll come back to haunt you and remind you of what was said
You'll stare never say never with a broken mirror of dread

Forget this not about promises you make
Because by saying never ever, so much is at stake

Melanie E. Williams

It's Just a Fantasy

Bid
Bottled Message
Confess to Me
Crimson and Cream
Ecstasy
Erotic or Not
Faceless
Midnight Train
Passion's Prison
REMs
Smile for Me
That Knight
X-Rated

"When a woman wants a man... the lover need
not bother to conjure up opportunities, for she will find
more in an hour than we men could think of in a century."

-Unknown

Bid

I like how you whisper tempting suggestions in my ear
Inviting me to partake in a love involving skin

A bid that's high and subsequently draws me nearer
Eliminating other options, so I gradually give in

Disappointed?

No.

Fulfilled?

Yes.

Try it again?

I think so.

Wanting more?

Nothing less...

Melanie E. Williams

"Gravitation cannot be held responsible
for people falling in love."

-Albert Einstein

Bottled Message

Dear Lover,

Upon the winds of affection soars a beating heart
Rapidly pulsating although we're miles apart
And did you know about a pair of kind eyes
desperately in search for her one true lover
somewhere upon God's lush earth?

My Delectable Lover,

I am searching for the stroke of your hands
To feel your touch, I'd walk across dunes of burning sand
Just to taste the sweetness in each tender kiss
Makes my heart pang because... it's your caress I miss

Dear Lover,

Should you find this poem bottled upon an ocean
Know that when I wrote it, you were the one
I was thinking of

"I love thee with the breath, smiles, tears, of all my life! And, if
God choose, I shall but love thee
better after death."

-Elizabeth Barrett Browning

Confess to Me

Tell me how my love makes you
comprise melodies of the wind
Or how your heart entangled
in fire bravely deepens

Tell me that life is unbearable
without my hand to hold
And how you'd love to pierce my soul
with a love that cannot be sold

Tell furtively your inner passions
that paint a picture unseen
About secret desires for me
that have kept you in wanting

Whisper to me with tender kisses
I am the one you invariably inhale
Then force me into a rapture that
allows our bodies to exhale

What do you confess my love?
With yearning I crave to know
Express to me private thoughts
that prompt your love for me to flow

Melanie E. Williams

"License my roving hands, and let them go,
before, behind, between, above, below."

-John Donne

Crimson and Cream

Crimson and red dripped with sweat and cream
The movements of our bodies
plunge for everything in between

Envision this sight with eyes tightly sealed
Fall into an abyss of secrets that doesn't seem real

Control the desire to make this moment end
Excite emotions that ascend and descend as we blend

No need to pinch yourself
It's reality and no dream
Your crimson and my red
dripped with your sweat and my cream

"Life has always taken place in a tumult without apparent
cohesion, but it only finds its grandeur and its reality
in ecstasy and in ecstatic love."

-Georges Bataille

Ecstasy

Have you ever loved someone so deeply
you could feel yourself drowning in bliss?
A love that feels so right always taking
you higher to give more and never less?

A love that extends to the heavens,
widths of continents, and depths of seas?
So powerful it can last an eternity?
One that erases all debt, forgives every
lie, pardons every injustice upon the soul?
Continuously cultivating that feeling
which never grows old?

A love that cannot be mapped nor designed?
Love not created by man but for man because
it surpasses the imagination of lovers
digging deeply within to uncover?

Have you ever wondered how it would feel
to love so real?

Ecstasy...

Melanie E. Williams

"Eroticism is like a dance: one always leads the other."

-Milan Kundera

Erotic or Not

When you slip your hands in a place that makes me sigh
licking cream from my lips and increasing my high

I think that's very very hot; erotic or not
You seem to warm me up in the right spot

Shadow boxing on a balmy, rainy night
You're just all over me; we're skin tight

Mmmmm yeah, that makes me rock. Erotic or not
To feel you taking jabs at me makes me so hot

I don't care what others may think
Any day of the week I will flock

To wherever you may be; erotic or not
I think you are so hot!

"It is the dim haze of mystery that adds enchantment to pursuit."

-Antoine Rivarol

Faceless

I once met a man with no face
All I had was his words to trace

His personality and his body in my mind
The unknown helped me to create an outline

Of what he was about; the totality of his depth
The mystique of him could keep me at bay...except

When I'm breathing quietly on the edge of night
Imaginations of him whisks me to a searchlight

Where he stands waiting to take me in his arms
My unseen man now takes on a life form

Finally, I can see him; that face... so beautiful... so strong
I wanted nothing more than to kiss him all night long

And manipulate my body to wrap him around me nice and tight
But my dream was interrupted by the sprinkling of sunlight

So as I stand watching the shower head making me wet
I think about the faceless man I never met...

At least not yet

Melanie E. Williams

"What is now proved was only once imagined."

-William Blake

Midnight Train

I close my eyes then you take me to that place;
That keeps me in agony before you begin to taste.

Tender succulent portions of my feminine loins;
Screaming for you to come inside and join me...

By entering into my cozy chamber of flurry;
Where you may take time to abide and bury.

Treasures that once remained secret;
But, no more Romeo 'cause I'm your Juliet.

Tonight, we leave Verona. Tonight, we'll make love on the
midnight train to Spain;
Do you think you can sustain?

From bringing the Earth to an abrupt, complete stop?
By holding tightly to each sweet gratifying drop?

Until I release the gates that secures my silky rivers;
Will you deliver...

Promised compositions of love-making and sweat;
That I sing as your tongue travels my spine. Are we there yet?

Mmmmm this train is moving full throttle to its
designated station;
Our thoughts are about to be freed from our imaginations.

Because we've finally arrived to the place of our dreams
Your crimson. My red. Your sweat. My cream.

"Our passions are like convulsion fits,
which, though they make us stronger for a time,
leave us the weaker ever after."

-Alexander Pope

Passion's Prison

When I look into your eyes I see over
the hills and passed the horizon
I am beguiled by the intense pleasure of your being
and locked away into passion's prison

Taking deep breaths of intoxicating
desire doesn't exactly free me
If the truth be told, I want to stay inside
of you and you inside of me for eternity

Undeniable joy is found in moments
we are fused in a silent dance
Executing the art of making love
I find not to be coincidence

Lover to lover, soaking skin,
pounding hearts, frenzied hips
Release me sweet lover so that I can again
return to passion's grip

Melanie E. Williams

"Dreams are true while they last,
and do we not live in dreams?"

-Alfred, Lord Tennyson

REMs

Satisfy my quiet soul by taking me to a place
that can only be penetrated through dreams

Visions of your fingertips, my breathy lips, and
our expressions filled with concentration
There's no sound
only the flickering of frames replayed
in my sub-consciousness

Eyes rapidly moving as I
silently watch passionate scenes
suspended in the center of my memory

Sweat softly lands on the tips of my lashes
and without thought...my smile arises with the sun

Now, I can clearly see what charcoaled skies
have brought forth is pure radiance

"A smile is a light in the window of the soul
indicating that the heart is at home."

-Unknown

Smile for Me

Smile for me when you feel the
intensity of the sun drenching every
crevice of your being, or when you think of
my tongue etching your spine
smile

When autumn's cool breeze
dances across your eyelashes, kisses
your lips, and then slowly moves on
When you savor the earth's salt, remember
the taste of my skin in a moment of
fire and then smile

If you feel yourself subsiding within,
think about the deepness of my sensuality and
how you were able to pull yourself out
only to go deeper once more and smile

Think of the beauty in my eyes, the
might of our desires when we blend
Consider the meeting of our minds in
a world so sublime and expose
the vitality of grace

Smile... for me

Melanie E. Williams

"No sooner met but they looked; no sooner looked but they
loved; no sooner loved but they sighed. No sooner sighed but
they asked one another the reason; no sooner knew the reason
but they sought the remedy."

-William Shakespeare

That Knight

Follow my thoughts carefully into a secured quiet place
Where my knight had a castle lanced with kisses
I mean it was laced

With touches of love everywhere that I walked
The message was vivid and he needed not talk

Candles lit to softly accent my knight
Mixed with the smell of his skin made it twice as nice

The conversation was sweet
but his lips tasted better
Tepidity produced dew upon our skin
We matched the weather

To see the look in his eyes as he savored my frame
Ended the division that made us twain
we became one in the same

Follow me quickly before this romantic moment ends
As our bodies ceased to ascend and descend

To when he fed my lips with delicacies so tender
Exit now my thoughts about that knight I remember

"We that are true lovers run into strange capers."

-Williams Shakespeare

X-Rated

There he is...standing before my very eyes. My dream. My love. I've been wanting so long for a man as lovely as you. And so, here you are. Not galloping upon a white horse. No. No armor. No javelin. Just my man. Pure and uncut.

The smell of your skin makes me feel loose. And I'm so opened to you when you're tasting my juice. And when your powerful hands grip my backside, I release mad screams the pillow fights to hide.

(Laughing) I'd better stop. This is getting way too x-rated. It's okay because when I lay down this pen, we're going to re-define adulterated.

See, it's been a long time and we need to release... that raging ball of love and desire we call the lust beast.

Index

Index

Abyss of Love, 72

Affirmations for the Woman in the Mirror, 39

All Caught Up, 73

Angel Friend, 40

As If I Were a Queen, 41

Bagged Dreams, 7

Beatings behind My Fence, 8

Before the Beginning, 23

Bid, 93

Bottled Message, 94

Buried, 74

Captured, 75

Cocooned, 9

Confess To Me, 95

Creating In Rain, 42

Crimson & Cream, 96

Deck, 43

Dehumanized, 10

Desperados, 58

Don't Speak, 24

Ecstasy, 97

Erotic or Not, 98

Evaporated, 25

Exception, 59

Faceless, 99

Faces of Feign, 60

Faded Expression, 11

Falling With Frailty, 12

First, Touch Me There, 26

Forgery, 61

Go Ahead, 44

Gold Digger, 62

Good Love, 76

Grape Cape, 45

Had It. Lost It., 27

He's Fixed, 77, 78

Him, 46

Index

I Think I Know You, 63
Inamorata, 64
Inked Emotions, 79
Just a Piece, 80
Krazed, 13
Lese' Maj'esty, 65
Lessons, 28
Let Me Peel This Off, 47
Lines, 66
Lost, 48
Love Fog, 29
Loveless Vertigo, 14
Me, 67
Midnight Train, 100
Mr. Big Man, 68
My Course of Time, 49
My Noble Man, 81
My Time, 82
Name That Addiction, 69
Not With My Tears, 15
Ode to a Lonely Soul, 16
Overflowin', 50
Passion's Prison, 101
Peep This...Twice, 83
Peer, 17
Question for Destiny, 30
Rainbows, 84
Rearview, 31
Reminisce This, 85
REMs, 102
Repeat That, 86
Rhythmic Love, 32
Rotations, 87
Sailing upon a Lover's Titanic, 18
Senses of Love, 51
Shades in My Mind, 52
Smile for Me, 103
Standin' Alone, 33
Strong, 53
Subjugation, 19
Summer of My Season, 54

Index

Swerve, 88
Taking Aim, 34
That Knight, 104
Think Only This of Me, 55
This Is Getting Old, 89
Unchained, 35
Us, 70
Wanting It Back, 36
What He Gets At Night, 20
While You Slept, 56
Winter Sensation, 90
Woman's Sorrow Part One, 21
Woman's Sorrow Part Two, 37
X Rated, 105
You Promise, 91

About the Author

Melanie E. Williams, a native of St. Louis, MO and a graduate of Missouri Baptist University, is an accomplished poet and educator. She has enjoyed traveling and living in different parts of the world with her family. She currently lives in Colorado.

www.ingramcontent.com/pod-product-compliance
Lightning Source LLC
LaVergne TN
LVHW091200080426
835509LV00006B/762